The Good and the Bad

This book belongs to

The Good and the Bad

A Youth's Guide for Recognizing Healthy Relationships

Sarah Hanley

SPIRITUAL FLOW
PUBLISHING

© 2023 Sarah Hanley

All rights reserved. No part of this publication may be reproduced, distributed, or transmitted in any form or by any means, including photocopying, recording, or other electronic or mechanical methods, without the prior written permission of the publisher, except in the case of brief quotations embodies in critical reviews.

Book formatting by Gareth Southwell
art.garethsouthwell.com

Published by Spiritual Flow Publishing

ISBN (hardback): 978-1-7750273-7-9
ISBN (paperback): 978-1-7750273-9-3
ISBN (ebook): 978-1-7750273-8-6

To Jenny

Thank you for the inspiration

and for all the lives you change

every day, just by being you!

Love you,

Sarah

From the moment you are born and placed in your mother's or guardian's arms, you begin to form a relationship.

Wanting to be in relationships is something that happens naturally. Every act of kindness, every hug or even the words you hear, help develop your beliefs about how you should be treated, and also about how you should treat others.

There are many different types of relationships that you can have over your lifetime. You have relationships with your family, friends, teachers, and even the ones you build with your pets. Some relationships are healthy and make you feel good, while others are unhealthy and make you feel bad.

Figuring out what type of relationship you have with others is important because it can affect how you feel. This will help you decide if you want to stay close to someone or keep your distance from them.

A healthy relationship is one where you feel like you are both benefiting from it equally. This means that you both feel like you are getting something good out of it, and you both have a say in what you want and need from each other. You are thoughtful and considerate of each other's feelings and try to make compromises when you disagree. You support each other and encourage each other to build each other up.

Knowing that you can be yourself in a relationship is very important. You have to feel comfortable with the other person and not feel like you have to change something about yourself for them to like you. If you try to change yourself for someone else, it can not only affect your other relationships but can also lead to you feeling bad about yourself. People who truly care about you will accept you as you are and appreciate all your perfections and imperfections.

In a healthy relationship, feeling safe and respected is a big deal. That means listening carefully to each other when something is bothering you and not trying to talk each other into things you don't want to do. You should always feel like your feelings and your body are protected when you're with someone you care about. This will allow you to let your guard down and have fun together!

The most important key in any relationship is TRUST. It ties in all of the elements of a healthy relationship. You have to trust the other person to be able to communicate and be honest with you, trust that you are always taking account of each other's feelings, and trust that you will respect and keep each other safe. It is important to always keep your promises and be able to depend on each other when you need to.

Overall, a healthy relationship with your friends and family should make you feel safe, loved, supported, and happy.

An unhealthy relationship with your friends and family might feel uncomfortable or even scary at times. These relationships can cause you to question yourself and your choices. They can keep you on edge and even lead to anxiety and stress.

When you feel like the person you have a relationship with is trying to control the things you do, how you act, or even what you wear, that is unhealthy. If they try to blame you when things go wrong and always make it feel like everything is your fault, that's unhealthy too.

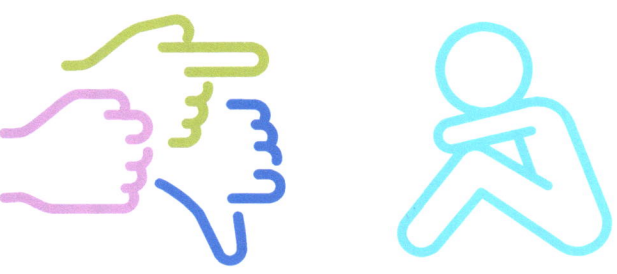

Gaslighting is when a person makes you doubt yourself, even when you know something is true. They do this to make you question yourself and feel guilty, and it is unhealthy. It's not okay for them to call you names or try to embarrass you in front of other people. Even if they say what they did was a 'joke', real friends don't make you feel less than to have a laugh or make themselves feel better.

Nobody should ever hurt you, whether it's by being mean to you or by physically hurting you. If someone is making you feel bad and pressuring you to do things you don't want to do, it's not okay, no matter what. You have the right to say no and to feel safe.

Sometimes, you are asked to hug or kiss a relative or friend goodbye. If it ever makes you feel uncomfortable, it's really important to let those around you know. You have the right to decide what feels right for you. Instead of a hug or kiss, you can give a high-five or a wave to say goodbye. Remember, nobody is allowed to touch you without your permission. You deserve to be treated with kindness and respect, no matter what!

Recognizing the difference between a secret and a surprise is also important. A secret is when you hide something from someone, while a surprise is when you hide something temporarily to make someone happy or excited. Never let anyone make you keep secrets from your parents or guardians because trustworthy people wouldn't ask you to do that. Your parents or guardians are there to protect you, so always share everything with them.

In any relationship, you should never feel scared of making the other person sad or angry when you are trying to talk to them honestly. Sometimes we even make excuses for the other person's behavior, as to why they acted a certain way or said hurtful things. However, in a healthy relationship, you shouldn't feel nervous or scared to be around the other person. If you ever feel like something isn't right, it's important to talk to a trusted adult or seek help from a teacher or counsellor.

There could be times you might find yourself in a situation you don't like and you need to get out of there, fast! One way to do this is to set up a 'safety net' for yourself, which is a person you trust to help you when you need it. You can call them or pick a special word or phrase to text your 'safety net', and they'll call you back right away to help you out of the crummy situation.

Another thing you can do is even practice saying "no" to different situations so you feel confident if you ever need to use it! And if you're still feeling unsure, you can also use an excuse like saying you have an upset stomach and need to go home. Most people can understand that, and you get to decide what feels good and safe for you.

The best part about growing up is that you get to decide who you let into your life and how they treat you. Even though you are taught to include everyone and be nice, which is important, you still get to choose who you let get close to you. Make a list of the traits that you think are important in a healthy relationship. For example, I love people who can make me laugh, so funny is an important trait to me.

- _____
- _____
- _____
- _____
- _____

- _____
- _____
- _____
- _____
- _____

When building healthy relationships, it's important to respect everyone's personal boundaries. Boundaries are like rules you make for yourself about how you want others to treat you. You can communicate your personal boundaries to your friends or family members and find out what theirs are too. It's okay if your boundaries are different from your friends' boundaries. If someone accidentally crosses your boundaries, you can politely let them know so that it doesn't happen again.

Let's celebrate the amazing healthy relationships you have in your life. Pick a parent, friend, or anyone else you have a healthy relationship with and show or tell them how much they mean to you.

Fun ways to do this are:

- Send them a text, letter, or thank you note to make them feel special.

- Draw or take a picture of you both and frame it for them.

- Think of a fun activity you could do together, like a picnic or play a game so you can spend time with them.

Relationships aren't always going to be perfect and sometimes they can feel like they are a lot of work but with the right people it can be worth it. That's why knowing how to recognize which relationships are healthy and unhealthy is so important. This way, you can decide who is worth putting your energy into.

Healthy relationships are ones that you can learn and grow with, leading to a stronger, happier, and healthier you!

About the Author

Over the last year, Sarah embarked on a transformative journey of self-love, which lead to a desire to share the valuable lessons she was learning with her children. With her books, her ultimate goal is to provide children with the necessary tools and inspiration to become the best versions of themselves. Through her writing, Sarah aspires to guide young readers towards embracing their unique qualities, fostering self-love, and empowering them with the confidence to navigate life's challenges.

Books

 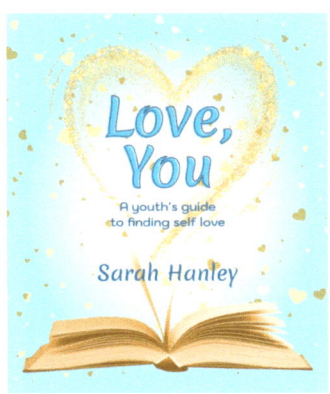 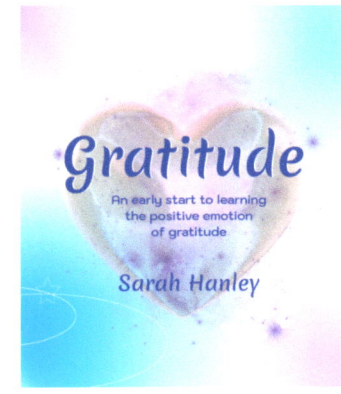

Journals

 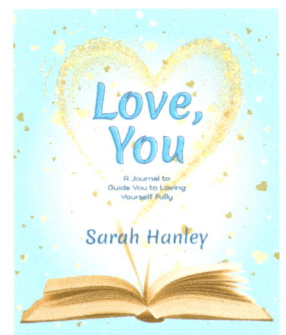 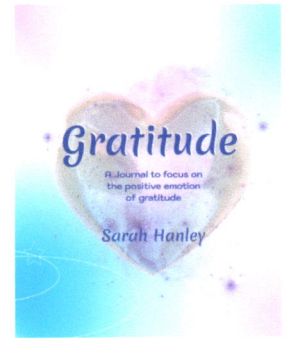

www.ingramcontent.com/pod-product-compliance
Lightning Source LLC
Chambersburg PA
CBHW042251100526
44587CB00002B/92